As We Remember
A History of the Woman's Relief Corps
In Beaufort, SC

As We Remember
A History of the Woman's Relief Corps
In Beaufort, SC

Najmah Thomas
Fred Washington, Sr.
Woman's Relief Corps No. 1 of SC

Fresh Ink Group
Guntersville

As We Remember
A History of the Woman's Relief Corps in Beaufort, SC

Fresh Ink Group
An Imprint of:
The Fresh Ink Group, LLC
1021 Blount Avenue #931
Guntersville, AL 35976
Email: info@FreshInkGroup.com
FreshInkGroup.com

Edition 1.0 2023

Cover by Stephen Geez / FIG
Book design by Amit Dey / FIG
Associate publisher Beem Weeks / FIG

Cataloging-in-Publication Recommendations:
HIS056000   HISTORY / African American & Black
HIS058000   HISTORY / Women
BIO023000   BIOGRAPHY & AUTOBIOGRAPHY / African American & Black
see Cultural, Ethnic & Regional / African American & Black

Library of Congress Control Number: 2023904569

ISBN-13: 978-1-958922-22-4 Papercover
ISBN-13: 978-1-958922-23-1 Hardcover
ISBN-13: 978-1-958922-24-8 Ebooks

Acknowledgements

This book would not be possible without the assistance
of the past and present members of Fred Washington, Sr.
Woman's Relief Corps No. 1 of SC.

For more information contact:
info@womansreliefcorpsbeaufort.org

Dedication

This book is dedicated in remembrance of
David Hunter No. 1, Beaufort (WRC).

Special thanks in remembrance of Ms. Margie Kline Jenkins,
founding member and President of the Beaufort County
Multicultural Association

Table of Contents

Introduction

"Though the battlefields are silent and ambulances have ceased their solemn rounds, though the battle-flags stained with the blood of the wounded are folded away and the mighty armies disbanded, the suffering caused by the civil war remains." WRC Department of Massachusetts, 1895

This book documents the remarkable story of a Woman's Relief Corps (WRC) chapter in Beaufort, South Carolina. The WRC is a national organization established as an official auxiliary to the Grand Army of the Republic (GAR) in 1883. The GAR stands out among groups that were created to ensure continuity of connection for veterans of the US Civil War; GAR posts served as crucial networks of moral support and fellowship for veterans after a traumatic war experience, and eventually as significant sources of political power. Similarly, as an auxiliary to the GAR, the WRC provided critical support to veterans in the form of nursing services, raising funds for much needed material goods for wounded and impoverished veterans and their families, and the intangible but impactful service of inspiring the patriotic cause after the war. With its motto of *fraternity, charity and loyalty*, the WRC distinguishes itself as the only patriotic group in the country founded 'solely on the basis of loyal womanhood, regardless of kinship' (WRC national statement, 2019).

A Woman's Relief Corps has existed in the city of Beaufort, South Carolina in various forms since 1892[1] when GAR Post David Hunter No. 9 (Post No. 9) was established in the city, with statesman Robert Smalls selected as Post Commander in 1894. Much of the record of the early Beaufort WRC was passed on through the oral history tradition, although National WRC Annual Convention records contain some directory level data on the activities of the GAR post and WRC auxiliary. With deep respect and appreciation to the oral tradition, this historical documentation is an effort to formally preserve and present a shared understanding of the Beaufort WRC's work conducted in service of the national corps' fraternity, loyalty and charity mission. It is written from the lived experiences and perspectives of past and present Corps members, with some supporting historical context provided.

Members of the WRC of Beaufort commissioned a study specifically for the purpose of ensuring their story is told for generations to come. That story intentionally centers African American women as lead agents of change, an important theme given the fact that historically the national WRC was White-led, and in southern localities like Beaufort, completely segregated. Beyond the Corps' primary purpose of documenting their work, this story is compelling as the nation contends with changing notions of its national identity and definitions of patriotism.

This book is written in testimony to the lives of each of the extraordinary women who comprised the WRC of Beaufort. Though some have passed on, and others have reached ages that render active service difficult, *the impact caused by the steadfast service of these women continues.*

---

[1] January 24, 1890 GAR Committee on Credentials of the Department of Georgia and South Carolina report – discussion of granting charters to organizations of colored veterans to form GAR Posts, recommendation that the David Hunter Post be transferred to the Department of Virginia, due to strong opposition in other southern posts to inclusion of colored members. Final vote resulted in the charter of David Hunter Post #29 in Beaufort SC under the GA and SC Department; the number was changed to Post #9 in 1889.

Historical Summary of the Beaufort Woman's Relief Corps, 1889-1996

"There are many people who do not know what some of the colored women did during the war. There were hundreds of them who assisted the Union soldiers by hiding them and helping them to escape. I know what they went through, especially those black men, for the Confederates had no mercy on them; neither did they show any toward the white Union solders. I have seen the terrors of that war. I was the wife of one of those men who did not get a penny for eighteen months for their services, only their rations and clothing." Susie King Taylor, 1902, Boston, MA

This chapter describes the founding years of the WRC in Beaufort, SC, setting it in the context of US Civil War and Reconstruction Era. The chapter includes biographical summaries of Harriet Tubman, Charlotte Forten Grimké and Susie King Taylor, due to their historic connections with Beaufort and the WRC. Harriet, Charlotte and Susie's experiences highlight the themes of entrepreneurial spirit, self-help, and financial support of families. They also amplify the distinct record of teaching, nursing, feeding and leading that Black women in Beaufort established during the Civil War and Reconstruction Era.

Harriet Tubman, Charlotte Forten Grimké, Susie King Taylor and the WRC

To tell a story of the founding of the WRC of Beaufort, we must of course bring to mind the US Civil War in Beaufort, because the WRC formed as a support group for the GAR, which formed as a support group for Civil War veterans. An examination of the lived experiences of Black women in Beaufort during the war will deepen and broaden our understanding about their actions after the war. In the majority of literature concerning the war, the southern Black woman's experience is often limited to their existence as enslaved, runaways, or 'contrabands of war,' or in some other instances as "the usual assortment of laundresses, cooks, and nurses" (Larson, 2004, p 211). However, Black women in and around Beaufort played a variety of essential roles during the Civil War, and those experiences likely influenced their post-war activities that led to the formation of the Beaufort WRC. The first-hand stories of antebellum southern Black women were rarely documented in detail, but notable exceptions include relatively widespread knowledge about the Civil War experience of Harriet Tubman, and perhaps less well-known, that of Charlotte Forten Grimké and Susie King Taylor. An examination of these key figures provides support for the thesis that Black women in Beaufort were far more than just victims of oppression and silent partners to the marginalized men in their lives.

We owe a debt of gratitude to those whose efforts went a long way towards counteracting attempts to obscure Harriet Tubman's significant influence on the American story before, during and after the US Civil War. Often known for her daring work in helping individuals and families to escape the bondage of slavery, there is now broader knowledge that Harriet also played a crucial role in Beaufort during the war. Evidence documents her arrival in Beaufort during March of

1862, upon recommendation from the Governor of Massachusetts.[2] Harriet would have been around 40 years old at the time, having embarked upon her journey as self-emancipator and Underground Railroad conductor more than 12 years prior. From the moment she arrived on the scene in Beaufort, Harriet took on multiple responsibilities of direct and indirect importance to the war effort. She was placed in charge of the distribution point set up by the YWCA to ensure Union soldiers received food, clothing, and books; and, she set up a washhouse and provided essential guidance for other Black women in Beaufort on how they could parlay their laundry, sewing and cooking skills into wages to support themselves and their families.

Image source: public domain

---

[2] John Andrew arranged for Harriet Tubman to travel to South Carolina in support of the Union War effort (Larson, P203-204)

Harriet served in the role of nurse to wounded soldiers, and those who fell ill due to a host of environmental factors. She recruited men to serve in the newly formed all-Black regiments, during a time when many were reluctant to join the Union effort. Harriet also planned and led execution of the decisively successful Combahee River Raid under General Montgomery, landing her in the pages of history as the only women (of any race) to lead a battle in the US Civil War.

Beaufort College Building (USCB campus) – former site of
Union Hospital during the Civil War
(image source: www.scencyclopedia.org/sce/entries/beaufort)

Larson summarizes Harriet's tenure in Beaufort[3] this way: "A cook and a laundress one day, a spy the next, Tubman continuously reinvented herself, adapting to and accommodating the immediate requirements of wartime crises with stunning success." (p. 212).

It is no surprise that Harriet appears in the journal pages of Charlotte Forten Grimké, the only free Black woman from the north who journeyed south in order to teach formerly enslaved Africans in 1862. Born without the weight of enslavement, Charlotte was a member of a wealthy family of free Blacks from Philadelphia. Her lineage included a long line of Revolutionary War veterans, successful businessmen, and staunch abolitionists.[4]

In the context of the Beaufort story, Charlotte is doubly unique because she is a free and wealthy Black woman who also had the presence of mind and skills to document her own story, which she did through her personal journal and a series of articles published by the *Atlantic Monthly*. A teacher by training, Charlotte arrived in Beaufort late October of 1862, at 25 years old. Her preparation for the task at hand included a Quaker education in Salem, Massachusetts, (she mastered French, German, and Latin) and tenure as the first Black woman hired to teach White students in Salem.

Keeping in the abolitionist tradition of her family line, Charlotte longed to do more in support of enslaved people in the south. After months of attempting to secure approval from the Port Royal Commission, she received word in September 1862

---

[3] Tubman's life spans 91 years, and historians document that she engaged fully as leader in the movement for women's suffrage well into her senior years.

[4] Charlotte's grandfather James Forten was a Revolutionary War soldier, a successful sailmaker, and one of the most prominent abolitionists of his time. Charlotte's father, Robert Bridges Forten was the first Black man buried with full military honors. Forten, P.219

that despite the safety concerns[5], the Commission was willing to support her as a missionary teacher in Beaufort District.

Charlotte joined White missionaries and founders of the Penn School on St. Helena Island, Laura Towne and Ellen Murray in October 1862. Her role would include far more than the teaching experience she had in Salem. Charlotte was charged with providing education to the children of formerly enslaved Sea Islanders in all subjects. During this time, she had the opportunity to engage on a different level with members of the formerly enslaved community, owing to her status as the only Black teacher at Penn School. She even worked in a general store some afternoons[6].

It is through Charlotte's documentation of life on the Sea Islands that we also learn of Black women like 'Old Suzy', who was "steeped in medicinal folklore and over the years had healed many sick people with her homemade brews and potions." Her memoirs also give us some insight into the balance of leadership immediately prior to the war.[7]

Charlotte's account also allows for deeper consideration of the work that Black women of Beaufort would have conducted while so many of the men in their families were absent due to engagement in the war effort. During the final days of her service at the Penn School, Charlotte finally got a chance to meet Harriet, whom she had desired to meet for a while. Charlotte's words underscore the impact of the meeting this way, "How I admired this heroic woman! How glad I was to have shaken her hand!" (196).

----

[5] "at any cost I *will* go" p139

[6] Forten, P. 164.)

[7] "Under slavery women had dominated. They cared for the cabin, bore and disciplined the children… On most plantations women went after the weekly and monthly rations meted out by the overseer. Women ground the family supply of corn and prepared the food; women received the ration of cloth and manufactured the necessary garments." Forten, .P174

Although Charlotte's work was conducted primarily on St. Helena Island (Oaklands, Seaside, Frogmore and the Corners), she frequently visited Beaufort, and it was during one of those trips when she had a chance to spend time with Harriet. Charlotte had non-social visits to Beaufort as well, serving as a nurse and stenographer for wounded soldiers following the disastrous battle at Fort Wagner that claimed the lives of her dear Col. Shaw and so many others in the 54th Massachusetts Volunteers. Although she does not mention her name

Susie King Taylor in 1902
(image source: Library of Congress)

directly, it is very possible that Charlotte crossed paths with Susie King Taylor during this time.

Like Harriet, Susie King Taylor, née Susan Ann Baker, was born into slavery, but she was taught to read and write due to the strategic relationships her grandmother developed throughout her formative years[8]. Owing to her early schooling,

---

[8] Although it was illegal at the time to teach Black residents to read and write, King Taylor's grandmother effectively leveraged the 'warm relationship' status between herself and the family that enslaved her family over the years, in order to send her granddaughter to some of the first freedom schools in Savannah, GA.

Susie was able to carefully document her own experience in Beaufort during the Civil War.

In her memoirs, Susie paints a vivid picture of a woman who was actively engaged in the war process. She recounts how being in the care of her uncle brought her from slavery in Liberty County to freedom in Savannah (Georgia), and then to the front lines of the war in Port Royal Island, Beaufort District. Susie makes regular note of her service to the Black men of the 54th Massachusetts Volunteers, who were stationed in and around Beaufort. One of Susie's essential roles in this area during the Civil War was that of teacher, despite the fact that she was only 15 years old. Her teaching skills were discovered during the trip by boat from Savannah to Beaufort, by General David Hunter (commander of the Union Forces in the Department of the South).

Susie was given charge over teaching children (about 40) and adults during her stay in Beaufort. Her memoirs show that by October 1862, she was located in Beaufort at Camp Saxton with her husband in Company E, where she worked as a laundress. Susie's husband was one of many Black soldiers who fought the Civil War on behalf of the Union for nearly two years without receiving pay.[9] Her work as a laundress was likely the primary source of income supporting their family during that time. This is an example of the "Black women's historic connection in shared struggle to men, children and community" (Cummings & Latta, 2010, p668).

Susie's memoir shows an entrepreneurial reaction to oppression and describes how Black women in Beaufort used their skills to support their families (including

---

[9] Black Civil War soldiers were initially paid half the amount of White soldiers. Instead of accepting the half-pay, the Black soldiers refused, and waited for the army to provide them with full pay (and back pay for the full amount) in 1864. Some soldiers died before receiving their pay, and having no documented heirs, had accounts that were not ever settled.

husband soldiers): "A great many of these men had large families, and as they had no money to give them; their wives were obliged to support themselves and children by washing for the officers of the gunboats and the soldiers, and making cakes and pies which they sold to the boys in camp" Taylor, p42.

A tradition of using entrepreneurship as the primary way to combat oppression can be understood by Susie's description of her mother and grandmother who were both business and landowning women[10]; it is clear that she learned skills and industriousness from their examples. This tradition of the entrepreneurial spirit, self-help, and financial support of families on the part of Black women in Beaufort is important in the larger story of their post-Civil War experience, and the overall record of service for the WRC of Beaufort.

Though distinctly different in age and experience, Harriet, Charlotte and Susie share a number of similarities in terms of their roles and their backgrounds. While Forten is not documented as having any formal role with the WRC, both Tubman and King Taylor are each directly linked with the organization; Tubman is noted as a member of the WRC in Auburn, NY, and after years of attempting to secure critically-needed backpay for her work conducted during the Civil War, she finally received her pension, in part as a result of the WRC's support for the Nurses Pension Act of 1892. King Taylor dedicates a chapter in her memoirs to the WRC, noting that she was responsible for organizing the WRC Chapter 67 where she served in various leadership roles, to include president in 1893[11].

Beyond the spectacular heroism of Harriet, the singularity of Charlotte's role as the only Black teacher at the first school for Africans who were enslaved in and around Beaufort, and the serendipitous placement of Susie on the

[10] King Taylor, p 124
[11] King Taylor, p 133

front lines of the War with the skills to document it, there is a thread of connection between their documented experiences and those of countless Black women in Beaufort who engaged in essential activities during the Civil War. Harriet, Charlotte and Susie where not the only Black women in Beaufort who risked their freedom to teach others; they were not the only ones who, through various entrepreneurial efforts such as cooking and cleaning, shouldered the financial burden for their families when Black soldiers went unpaid; they were not the only ones who used their knowledge of local herbs to nurse wounded soldiers; and they were not alone in their efforts to bring food and relief to imprisoned Union soldiers, despite the penalty.[12] As Susie King Taylor notes, there were 'hundreds of them;' and for these and other Black women in Beaufort, a distinct record of teaching, nursing, feeding, and leading that was forged during the Civil War served as a foundation for the Woman's Relief Corps of Beaufort.

Black women of Beaufort continue service after the Civil War

Robert E. Lee's surrender to Ulysses S. Grant at Appomattox Courthouse on April 9, 1865 ended the War; the reality of the war recovery effort was that resources of communities on all sides were stretched precariously thin. In the war's wake remained thousands of wounded soldiers, as well as surviving widows and orphans. It is important to consider that there was no national entity in place to meet the needs of these often indigent citizens, to say nothing of the newest group of citizens—African Americans—who were finally able to cast

---

[12] "The Union soldiers were in it, worse than pigs, without any shelter from sun or storm, and the colored women would take food there at night and pass it to them, through the holes in the fence. The soldiers were starving, and these women did all they could toward relieving those men, although they knew the penalty, should they be caught giving them aid." Susie King Taylor, p 142; see also James McPherson's account of 'secret helpers,' p150 MacPherson, James, *The Negro's Civil War* (New York, 1965)

away previous titles and conditions of 'slave,' 'runaway,' 'contraband,' and 'free-man,' owing to the Civil War/Reconstruction Amendments.[13]

The war effort transitioned into a sustained relief effort on the part of many through informal and formal organizations, such as the GAR. The GAR was created to ensure continuity of connection for veterans of the US Civil War. It was founded in Decatur, Illinois a few days short of the 1st anniversary of the war's end, on April 6, 1866, and very quickly became the most prominent organization for Civil War Veterans.[14] All across the nation, GAR posts served as crucial networks of moral support and fellowship for veterans. By 1890, the GAR boasted 409,489 members with a post located in every state in the nation. Although the national WRC was organized prior to the end of the war in 1863, it was established as an official auxiliary to the GAR in 1883. Both entities were organized in departments at the state level with several numbered (and often named, after a deceased veteran) local chapters referred to as 'posts,' with attached WRC posts.

By 1886, Susie King Taylor had relocated from Beaufort to Boston, Massachusetts where she helped to organize WRC Post 67 on February 25[15]. Three years later on

---

[13] The 13th Amendment abolished slavery (except as punishment for crime), the 14th Amendment extended Due Process and Equal Protection, and the 15th Amendment granted African American men the right to vote. Reconstruction is noted by many historians as the period between 1865-1876 where efforts focused on rebuilding the South's infrastructure and economy, as well as transition millions of formerly enslaved Africans to citizenship.

[14] "Membership was limited to honorably discharged veterans of the Union Army, Navy, Marine Corps or the Revenue Cutter Service that served between April 12, 1861 and April 9, 1865. Almost every prominent veteran was enrolled, including five presidents: Grant, Hayes, Garfield, Harrison, and McKinley. In its early days, the GAR limited its activities merely to fraternal activities. But soon, members began discussing politics in local gatherings. A growing interest in pensions signaled the beginning of open GAR participation in national politics. The rank and file soon realized the value of presenting a solid front to make demands upon legislators and congressmen. The GAR become so powerful that the wrath of the entire body could be called down upon any man in in public life who objected to GAR-sponsored legislation." LOC, GAR, September 13, 2011.

[15] Robert A. Bell Corps 67, Boston, MA. https://archive.org/stream/historyofdepartm01woma/ historyofdepartm01woma_djvu.txt

April 22, 1889, the WRC of Beaufort was established as the auxiliary to GAR Post David Hunter No. 9[16] and records suggest King Taylor was one of the original organizers. According to a national WRC report, by the year ending October 1, 1890 the Beaufort WRC, led by its president Susan M. Wallace, had 28 members who paid $1 in membership dues annually. While a relief fund was not yet established at that time, WRC of Beaufort was the only Corps noted in South Carolina, and one of the few in the south for several years.

Much of the record of the early Beaufort WRC was passed on through the oral history tradition; however, owing to documentation of all Corps and Detached Corps associated with the National WRC, there is a substantial amount of information available about the organization's official records. The National WRC reports relating to the proceedings of its National Conventions from 1884 through 1981 contain information about the WRC of Beaufort. Even at the outset when African American posts were deemed 'detached corps' by the national group (due to Jim Crow segregation), they still provided detailed records, reports and dues to the national WRC. The WRC of Beaufort adhered to all requirements of the National WRC, such as hosting regular meetings, observing rituals (including reciting the charter at each meeting), reading of national orders, compiling and submitting reports and dues, and reviewing rules and regulations by all members. These historical records, combined with the individual and collective memories of Beaufort WRC members offer important messages for our current context, and guideposts for our future.

---

[16] Post No. 9's namesake, Major General David Hunter endeared himself to African Americans in Beaufort, owing in part to his initial emancipation of enslaved in the Military Department of the South (SC, GA & FL) via General Order No. 11, as well as his leadership of the 1st SC Volunteer Regiment of colored troops.

Woman's Relief Corps of Beaufort

Timeline of Key Events

US Civil War (1861-1864)

- April 12, 1861 – Confederates fire on Fort Sumter; US Civil War begins
- October 1862 – Susie King arrives at Camp Saxton, Charlotte Forten arrives at Penn Center
- January 1, 1863 – Emancipation Proclamation read at Camp Saxton
- June 1863 - Harriet Tubman leads Combahee River Raid
- April 9, 1865 – US Civil War Ends

Reconstruction (1865 - 1877 / 1878 - 1900)

- May 1, 1865 – 1st Decoration Day in Charleston, SC
- December, 1865 – 13th amendment abolishes slavery in the US, except as punishment for a crime
- 1866 – Grand Army of the Republic (G.A.R) formed
- 1868 – P. Allen's Brass Band formed; Robert Smalls elected to SC House of Rep; General Logan's Memorial Day Order issued
- 1869 – First Woman's Relief Corps (WRC) chapter established
- 1873 – Parris Island legislation

Early WRC Era (1901 - 1940)

- 1881 – Beaufort WRC Chapter recorded
- 1883 – National WRC becomes G.A.R Auxiliary
- 1886 – Susie King Taylor forms WRC 67
- 1889 – G.A.R David Hunter Post 9 established
- 1895 – SC Convention—school segregation & disenfranchisement for SC African Americans
- 1896 – Plessy v Ferguson Supreme Court case
- 1897 – Julia Layton elected National Inspector for Grand Army Hall (G.A.H) dedicated to Beaufort WRC Southern Post

Jim Crow / Segregation

- 1911 – Julia Layton visits WRC of Beaufort
- 1918 – Shift in Beaufort's Black population begins; end of WWI
- 1920 – 19th amendment, woman's suffrage
- 1929 – Great Depression
- 1939 – WWII
- 1940 – Zora Neal Hurston records at Commandment Keeper Church service at Beaufort G.A.H

Civil Rights Era (1941 - 1964 / 1965 - 1995)

- 1944 – Mabel Staupers, RN leads efforts to allow Black nurses in the US Army
- 1946 – 1st Presidential Committee in Civil Rights
- 1948 – President Truman orders desegregation of US Armed Forces
- 1954 – Brown v Board Supreme Court case
- 1964 – Beaufort County integrates public schools

Modern WRC Era

- May 1989 – Beaufort County Department of Veterans Affairs publishes Memorial Day history
- October 1986 – Grand Army Hall Historic Preservation Fund incorporated in Beaufort, SC; building restored, rededication ceremony May 30, 1988
- May 1976 – final 'Decoration Day' Celebration in Beaufort, SC

Present Day (1996 - current)

- 1996 – Beaufort WRC reorganization begins
- 1998 – Beaufort WRC renamed in honor of Fred Washington, Sr.
- 2013 – The Fred Washington, Sr. Woman's Relief Corps #1 recognized by SC House Resolution 4110, incorporated as 501(c)3 organization
- 2019 – Historical documentation project begins

Timeline periods: 1861-1864 | 1865-1877 | 1878-1900 | 1901-1940 | 1941-1964 | 1965-1995 | 1996-current

In Service:
The Ongoing Work of the
Woman's Relief Corps

"In the beginning I wish to express my appreciation of having been honored with the office of Assistant National Inspector, and while I appreciate the honor, I prize more the opportunity that was given to me to help the Corps of my own race." Julia Mason Layton of Potomac, 1911 – WRC Convention Address

This chapter describes the WRC motto, mission, badge, and related ceremonial items. It sets the tone of patriotism that was so important to the work of WRC members and provides important information from the Black woman's perspective on patriotism, including their work to support patriotic education for Beaufort County school students and community members. The Chapter details the specific work of the Beaufort WRC in terms of service to the general public during annual ceremonies with a particular focus on Decoration Day (currently known as Memorial Day), as well as its ongoing relief efforts for elderly and disabled veterans. This chapter also contextualizes the history of the Beaufort WRC as an all-Black Corps supporting the patriotic cause in a southern locality governed by Jim Crow segregation laws and norms.

A badge and a charge

As an auxiliary to the GAR, the WRC extended the wartime service rendered by women loyal to the Union. WRC posts provided critical support to veterans in the form of nursing services, raising funds for much needed material goods for wounded and impoverished veterans and their families, and the intangible but impactful service of creating the patriotic cause after the war. With its motto of *fraternity, charity and loyalty*, the WRC distinguishes itself as the only patriotic group in the country founded 'solely on the basis of loyal womanhood, regardless of kinship.'[17] National WRC records show 130,789 members in good standing as of June 30, 1892, in 2,356 posts across the country.

The official badge of the WRC is a Maltese Cross of copper bronze, containing the GAR medallion; at the center of this badge are the Statue of Liberty, a Soldier, a Boy, a Woman, a Child, and the American Flag, all contained inside a wreath of stars (see figure)[18]. According to the national WRC description, the figure of the soldier references

---

[17] There were other groups at the national level recognized as auxiliary to the GAR; these groups included women's groups, but the WRC was the only group that did not require some form of hereditary ties to a Civil War Veteran. LOC

[18] Woman's Relief Corps, retrieved 5/18/2002 from http://suvcw.org/wrc.htm

fraternity with 'comrades' in the GAR, the boy represents youth and strength of the future for the country, the child reflects hope that freedom and justice for the future will prevail through patriotic teachings of loyalty, and the woman symbolizes motherhood as the course of all civilization—teaching mercy and kindness, extending charity throughout the world. From its inception until present day, a detailed set of rules, regulations and rituals has prescribed the work of the WRC at the national level; these requirements are promulgated in turn to each local post through their respective state departments.

The WRC has three primary objectives: (1) to perpetuate the memory of the Grand Army of the Republic through specific activities: Memorial Day, Lincoln's Death Day Commemoration, Gettysburg Remembrance Day, Living Memorials, National Holidays, and Maintenance of GAR Memorial Museums, (2) to assist veterans, their widows and orphans through Hospital Volunteer Service, Active Soldiers, Legislation, Red Cross, Local Community Services, Scholarships, Child Welfare, Narcotic Prevention and Education, and Libraries; and (3) to promote patriotism in our country through Patriotic Education, Etiquette of the Flag, Americanization, National Defense, and Schools/Education Programs. National rules prescribe election of a president, senior and junior vice president, secretary/treasurer, deputy treasurer/assistant secretary, chaplain, inspector, counselor, field officer, patriotic instructor, press correspondent and senior aide. The target audience for the WRC's efforts to promote patriotism included adult members of the community as well as school-aged members. For example, WRC members were responsible for visiting each school in Beaufort to provide instruction on how to properly decorate graves in the National Cemetery with the US flag.

HONORING THE DEAD AT SEA Members of the Black Community of Beaufort carry out the annual throwing of flowers to sea honoring the dead who lost their lives at sea. The ceremony is carried out by the community each year the week before Memorial Day. This year it was held at the foot of the Freedom Mall boat ramp. (Photo by Bob Carpenter)

Beaufort WRC members lead children during Memorial Day event – May 1970

Decorating freedom

In terms of community-wide events to 'perpetuate the memory of the Grand Army of the Republic', the Beaufort WRC's celebrations of Memorial Day—also known as Decoration Day—is recalled by members as their signature affair. The WRC's longstanding role in organizing and presenting Memorial Day celebrations for Beaufort was recognized by the SC House Resolution 4110 on May 14, 2013[19].

Historian David Blight documented the first public recognition of honoring the nation's War dead in Charleston, SC on May 1, 1865. That day, 28 Black men (many who had been enslaved prior to the US Civil War) made proper graves for 257 Union soldiers who died fighting against the institution of chattel slavery; many had perished from disease and exposure while being held at a makeshift prison on the site of Charleston's once exclusive Washington Racecourse and Jockey Club.

After the men prepared proper resting places for the fallen soldiers, there was a grand parade of over 10,000 people (mostly Black Charlestonians) followed by decorations of grave sites at the new cemetery with flowers, hence the name 'Decoration Day.' The ceremony and gathering also included scripture readings,

---

[19] House Journal-page 12

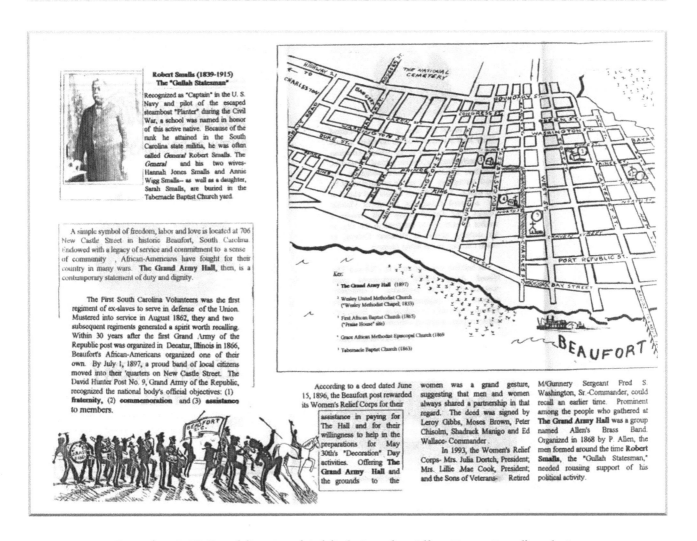

Beaufort WRC publication highlighting the Allen Brass Band's role in
Decoration Day Celebrations.

drill demonstrations, and picnic lunches on the field. It was a time for the Black community to offer gratitude for battles won and to build collective strength for battles to come. After that day, historians document that other cities and states across the country began to observe Decoration Day[20].

Decoration Day was especially prominent in the City of Beaufort, where so many Civil War soldiers are buried. Beaufort WRC members and others recount a

---

[20] "The Confederate organizations and other kind friends have joined us with true friendship every Decoration day in our celebration of that day, which is observed all over the Union." Davies, p. 357

three-day event that began with an influx of thousands of visitors by car, bus and boat on Saturday, a formal church program and processional to the Beaufort Bay to cast flowers on the water for fallen sailors on Sunday, and on Monday, a thrilling parade led by the Allen Brass Band followed by a day-long festival of food, fun and fellowship. The March 8, 1988 'Report of the Historical Committee for the Memorial Day Observation' prepared by Beaufort Councilman Leroy E. Brown is perhaps the most detailed account of Decoration Day ceremonies in the city. A copy of the committee report is available for download on the WRC's public history website (see Afterward for additional details). Even when the name shifted from Decoration Day to Memorial Day, in Beaufort the observation was largely a Black holiday, planned and executed by Black-led organizations like the WRC. This was likely due to the out-sized impact of Jim Crow segregation on the lived experiences of southern residents.

Serving those who served

The Beaufort WRC took seriously its charge to assist veterans, their widows and orphans. It is important to imagine the desperate circumstances endured by most, if not all, communities in the south immediately following the Civil War. In addition to mourning the loss of those who died during the war, communities and families had to shoulder the burden of wounded soldiers and also help meet the needs of those made widows and orphans as a result of the war. There was no local, state or federal department of social services or safety net programs we might be familiar with in existence during that time. Informal and formal community organizations had a significant role to play in relief not just immediately after the war, but in the longer term as well. Organizations like the WRC provided crucial social and financial support to veterans and their families by collecting dues from their membership and conducting fundraising activities to support their work. Some of the primary activities conducted by Corps members over the organization's more contemporary history include volunteer service at the Naval Hospital, the Red Cross, and other local community service organizations, raising funds and other necessary supplies for veterans residing at Victory House in Walterboro, SC, and providing scholarships to children of veterans.

Teach them to remember

The story of the WRC of Beaufort is a reminder that Black women in the South have carried the banner of patriotism since the country's founding and continue to do so in the present day. Although there are relatively few publications focused on the subject of Southern Black women and patriotism, historians like Breen (1978), Morgan (2005) and Clinton (2016) do address the matter in context. Breen discusses the attitudes of Black women in the South during WWI through an examination of the records by the Committee on Women's Defense Work. Evidence shows that Black women responded patriotically during the Great War, even while they expressed their dissatisfaction with official and nonofficial efforts to deliberately exclude them from participation in the war effort. Breen contends that Black women in the South "remained anxious to demonstrate their patriotism when given the opportunity." Morgan provides further support for the claim, describing how Southern Black WRC members were committed to the organization's mission of loyalty, even when their property and lives were threatened.[21]

Reciting the Pledge of Allegiance[22], saluting the Star-Spangled Banner, and singing the US National Anthem at major sporting events are some examples of symbols and rituals of patriotism that are intended to support a united identity. However,

[21] "In the face of threats to burn down their meeting hall, WRC members in Marche, Arkansas met in secret three miles into the woods." Morgan, F. 2005. Women and Patriotism in Jim Crow America, p97.
[22] The National WRC is documented as the first national organization to adopt and promote the Pledge of Allegiance in 1894. Their efforts sparked a nationwide adoption of this formalized salute to the flag.

the patriotic identity we know today did not happen spontaneously; it is the result of a decades-long campaign by a number of groups, including the Woman's Relief Corps. The WRC mission is clear about its intent to provide material aid to military soldiers and their families; however, the scope of this work expanded well beyond 'relief'. Perhaps one of the most long-lasting and consequential impacts of the WRC's service is related to the organization's third objective, promoting the patriotic cause after the US Civil War. Historian John C. Kennedy's dissertation "A Perfect Union: The Woman's Relief Corps and Women's Organizational Activism, 1861-1930," presents a detailed examination of the work conducted by the WRC at the national level in terms of patriotic civic activism.

A deeper understanding of patriotism is important to the story of the WRC of Beaufort, given the WRC's mission regarding patriotism and in light of the complex experiences of Black women and notions of patriotism. Parker (2010) makes a valuable distinction between two types of patriotism: blind and symbolic. Blind patriotism entails an 'uncritical support for national policies and practices,' whereas symbolic patriotism describes an "abstract, affective attachment to the nation and its core values" (p97). Dietz (2002) puts a finer point on the distinction, arguing that "true patriots are those who are both devoted to American political values and possess a critical understanding of them."

The 'and' in Dietz's distinction is especially important in the context of the story of the Woman's Relief Corp of Beaufort. Evidence suggests that Black WRC members adhered to and worked hard to spread symbolic patriotism not blind patriotism. Foundational support for this argument is available in the research on the development of blind patriotism; Smith (1988) contends this less critical form of patriotism evolved during the aftermath of the US Civil War, where love of country eventually became equated with "projecting American power and domination of 'others' and building the American empire."

Even as far back as the Revolutionary War, people of African descent in America found themselves at the intersection of patriotism and freedom; the story of the Black Loyalists provides important context for further understanding of dissent-based or symbolic patriotism and freedom.[23] Arguably, chattel slavery and Jim Crow segregation were key factors in the development of blind patriotism for some Americans, but Black citizens generally (and Black women, in particular) did not have the luxury to adopt this kind of patriotism due to their lived experiences as an excluded group.

The fact that Black men and women in Beaufort fought for the right to serve in the US armed forces further illustrates their commitment to symbolic patriotism. Despite their efforts, Black women were not officially allowed to serve as nurses in the army until 1945. Although military service was an important component of patriotism, it was not the only focus, especially for Black women. As Leslie A. Schwalm details in her book *A Hard Fight for We,* Black women in South Carolina played an active role in the ongoing struggle for full citizenship outside of the military arena. This work was often conducted in clubs and organizations such as the WRC of Beaufort.

As an organization formed shortly after the end of the Civil War, the WRC of Beaufort illustrates Schwalm's contention that Black Women in the South Carolina Lowcountry played an active role in public life and the social landscape during Reconstruction "as participants in the interrelated struggle to define freedom."[24]

---

[23] *The Book of Negroes: A Novel* by Lawrence Hill, tells the story of a woman Aminata Diallo who was abducted from her village in Africa, sold into slavery in South Carolina, and eventually forged her way to freedom by serving the British in the Revolutionary War and registering her name in the 'Book of Negros'. The Book of Negros is based on an actual document listing nearly 3,000 names of Black Loyalists; this register was created at the direction of Sir Guy Carleton, Commander-in-Chief of the British forces in North America, Sir Guy Carleton, during the British evacuation of New York on November 30, 1782. See https://www.bac-lac.gc.ca/eng/discover/military-heritage/loyalists/book-of-negroes/pages/introduction.aspx for more details. Lawrence's novel was also made into a six-part TV mini-series.
[24] Schwalm, L. (1997) p 7,

The Beaufort WRC used community-wide events (especially those events held during Memorial Day and Labor Day), distribution of educational materials, and service to veterans and their families as some of their main strategies for promoting the patriotic cause while serving their community.

The WRC and Jim Crow Segregation

Jim Crow, based on a caricature of Blacks used in minstrel shows, came to typify a broad body of laws that codified segregation of the races and resources in all public and private institutions and practices. While separation was the presenting character of segregation, the purpose was primarily about reinforcing notions of White superiority and Black inferiority in all facets of life in the South.[25] Black citizens in South Carolina enjoyed a brief window of political, social and economic gains between the end of US Civil War and Reconstruction,[26] but by 1895, South Carolina's constitutional convention had effectively denied the right to vote for most of the state's African American population and codified racial segregation with separate (and unequal) facilities, beginning with the public school system in 1895 and rail and other forms of transportation in 1898.

---

[25] "The Jim Crow laws gave new meaning and reinforcement to white supremacy, prescribing black access to places and things, to opportunities and to rights. Perhaps the color line's most insidious role was the ability to transform the very meaning of "We the people," despite monumental constitutional changes that had occurred during Reconstruction." Franklin, J. and Higginbotham, E. *From Slavery to Freedom: A History of African Americans.* p 261

[26] DuBois, W.E.B. (1903) Of the Dawn of Freedoms, in *Souls of Black Folks,* description of a key agency during Reconstruction, the Freedmen's Bureau, explains in part the ultimate failure of Reconstruction: "To understand and criticize intelligently so vast a work, one must not forget an instant the drift of things in the later sixties. Lee had surrendered, Lincoln was dead, and Johnson and Congress were at loggerheads; and all the Southern lad was awakening as from some wild dream to poverty and social revolution. In a time of perfect calm, amid willing neighbors and streaming wealth, the social uplifting of four million slaves to an assured and self-sustaining place in the body politic and economic would have been a herculean task; but when to the inherent difficulties of so delicate and nice a social operation were added the spite and hate of conflict, the hell of war; when suspicion and cruelty were rife, and gaunt Hunger wept beside Bereavement, - in such a case, the work of any instrument of social regeneration was in large part foredoomed to failure." P. 17.

Despite their ideals regarding fraternity, charity, and loyalty, and their distinction of being the only patriotic group in the country founded 'solely on the basis of loyal womanhood regardless of kinship', the national WRC experienced its share of racial tensions, and "unlike in the Grand Army, succumbed to pressure to segregate."[27] The National WRC practiced a form of 'decentralized segregation',[28] with racially integrated departments in the North and West, as well as segregated departments in the South.

Most Black WRC chapters reported directly to the National WRC as 'detached corps', instead of to their respective state departments. As Kennedy argues, the segregation of Black WRC corps suggested these members were considered to be inferior compared to the organization's White members. Minutes from various national WRC conference proceedings further highlight some negative and dismissive characterizations of Black WRC chapters, especially those in the South.

Evidence reveals the National WRC had a complicated relationship with its Black members, and especially those located in former Confederate states like South Carolina. Promoting the Union memory in these areas was difficult, especially in the face of the Lost Cause[29] ideology. Often, African American groups were the only ones that maintained Union cemeteries and displayed the American Flag

---

[27] Kennedy, p209

[28] "I describe this policy of racial separation as decentralized segregation because it was implemented in the southerner states only and not in the other regions of the country or at the national level." Kennedy, p. 211

[29] "For some Southerners, the Civil War was a noble "Lost Cause." This was once the reigning interpretation in the South and long influenced the historiography of the Civil War and its aftermath. The Lost Cause mythos itself has a history: it was a post-Reconstruction invention to explain defeat in the Civil War and maintain a whites-only political system. It was, as John A. Simpson tells it, a militant form of "Confederate nostalgia" that had by 1913 "permanently stamped the cult of the 'Lost Cause' upon the national character." The movie *Birth of a Nation* (1915) and the book (1936) and movie (1939) of *Gone With the Wind* were all popular cultural manifestations of this "cult." Retrieved on January 4, 2020 from https://daily.jstor.org/origins-confederate-lost-cause/

in these states.[30] The importance of Black members in the South was not lost on national WRC leaders, many of whom were northerners who opposed segregation. Despite the progressive stance of national WRC leaders and a good portion of their members (including, understandably, Black northern women), the organization adopted a policy of decentralized segregation for three primary reasons: paternalism, hostility, and expansion.

Paternalism was evident in some members' belief that Black WRC corps would not be able to complete the required paperwork or implement the various WRC rituals effectively, due in part to the high levels of illiteracy among Blacks in the south[31]. In terms of hostility, an examination of National WRC convention proceedings reveals that White southern WRC members simply refused to work with Black members on mission-related activities[32]. This refusal was less related to potential inability to conduct the WRC-specific work and more related to general notions about racial superiority that were the norm in southern society.

Similarly, the third reason for the National WRC's submission to segregation was the desire to grow its membership base in the South; the expected response that southern White women would refuse to associate with African American comrades undergirded the national WRC's adoption of decentralized segregation. The WRC's national vice-president articulated the conviction of many White members at the 1892 National Convention: "My experience has shown that, if a Colored Corps is organized in a town first, you will get no other."[33] So the National WRC's

---

[30] Davies, p370; Kennedy, p 210

[31] It is important to note here that illiteracy was a function of laws prohibiting Blacks from accessing education (at all, and then, on an equal basis), not a function of inherent inability; yet no distinction of this fact is made during arguments presented to support separating Black WRC chapters in the records available for review.

[32] Journal of the Tenth Annual Convention of the Woman's Relief Corps, Auxiliary to the Grand Army of the Republic, 1892, p 35; 492-493

[33] Ibid.

adopting of decentralized segregation was essentially a tradeoff—expansion of the WRC over equality for Black WRC members.

Julia Mason Layton ensures national support for the Beaufort WRC

There were some voices at the National WRC level who spoke against segregation in the organization, such as former president Annie Wittenmyer and member Julia Mason Layton, who would eventually be appointed as national inspector for the WRC's Black Corps in 1893. Layton was born into slavery in Virginia, but her father purchased her freedom during her early childhood after her mother's death. She worked as a teacher in Virginia and joined the WRC as the wife of a disabled navy veteran.[34]

The records suggest that Layton consistently spoke out against race prejudice and segregation in the National WRC; during the 1897 Convention, she reminded the membership she joined the WRC "with the understanding that it was the one organization on the face of the globe that accorded a woman her right, be she black or white."[35] She responded to criticism about Black WRC Corps' abilities by suggesting that the WRC members do more to improve the situation facing Black women in the South instead of simply maligning their character and ignoring their loyalty to the nation. During the 1911 Convention, she spoke more specifically about her motivation for serving in the role of inspector.

Layton's need to remind her comrades of the importance of equality, regardless of race, illustrates an ongoing disconnection between blind and symbolic patriotism for Black WRC members. Her efforts revealed the strength and dedication to patriotic ideals among Black WRC chapters in the South. In many

[34] Morgan, p38
[35] WRC 5th National Convention, 1897, p 323

Julia Mason Layton – April 25, 1903
(image source: The Colored American)

instances, Layton's reports to the National WRC from the Southern field clearly illustrated how they existed and persisted in a society that was determined to write them out of the nation's patriotic narrative and further entrench their third-class citizenship status.

The Beaufort WRC's work during the period of Jim Crow segregation (and the decentralized segregation within the National WRC) is testimony to the position that Black citizens, and Black women in particular, have long demonstrated an ability to 'negotiate the narrow strait'[36] of patriotism, promoting both love of country and actively participating in critical dissent to the country's inequalities of opportunities. It is important to place emphasis on the WRC of Beaufort's role as an African American Southern Woman's group, working to instill patriotism among people often denied the benefits of full citizenship.

By virtue of their previous condition of servitude, or in later years, exclusion from equal employment opportunities, Black WRC members were not likely

---

[36] Nussbaum, M.,P232

to be financially well-off. However, while many White southern women's clubs worked to maintain a state-supported social order predicated on White dominance over others, "at the same time and without state aid, black club women used their own resources to fund social welfare programs."[37] Similarly, they used their limited resources to memorialize the Union cause and spread patriotism in the Black community. For example, in the 1892 WRC National Convention records, the Beaufort WRC is listed as having the 3rd highest number of decorated graves for Union soldiers among the detached corps and 9th highest of all WRC corps—a total of 10,000 graves decorated by 51 of 67 of the Beaufort WRC members who were active at the time.[38]

Jim Crow segregation confronted Julia Mason Layton during the course of her official work inspecting and providing guidance to the detached corps in the South, including the Beaufort WRC. As Larson (p. 235) notes, "black women were not given the same courtesies and respect white women expected and were accorded in public (and some private) spaces, posing a special and particular kind of burden for them."

Layton described, in great detail, the harrowing events of her journey to remote locations in search of Black WRC corps; she was not allowed to ride in the 'ladies car' for the majority of her journey, could not secure appropriate overnight accommodations, and faced such dangers on her travels that she carried a 'six-shooter' for protection. One of her fellow WRC members noted, "You have no idea of the humiliation she was forced to endure and the hardships while in performance of her work."[39] Despite these hardships, Mason continued her work on behalf of the WRC's detached corps; her report at the 1911 National Convention

---

[37] Johnson, M. Drill into us...the Rebel Tradition: The Contest over Southern Identity in Black and White Women's Clubs in South Carolina, 1898-1930. The Journal of Southern History, 66:3. P527
[38] Journal of the ... Convention of the National Woman's ... v.10 (1892).
[39] WRC National 1911, p281

United States Colored Troop (USCT) grave marker at the Beaufort National Cemetery
image source: Najmah Thomas

clearly suggests that her motivation was related to the work being conducted by these women at the local level, despite the conditions imposed by Jim Crow laws:

"I may have given a longer account of the work of the Detached Corps than may seem necessary, but I feel all should know how much these isolated Corps are doing for the comrades in their declining years and for the cause of Patriotism. I, and the Assistant Inspectors, gleaned these facts when on our visit to these Corps, and in justice to them feel it my duty to let the members of the W.R.C. know what our distant coworkers are doing.

In many places they are working under most unfavorable conditions, and it is most discouraging, but a little band of heroic women here and there are trying to uphold the principles of our Order, to fulfill their obligation to the best of their ability, and for the love of the dear old flag, hold their charter, and keep on in the good work. Let us give them our sympathy and hearty cooperation." Layton, 1911

The record shows that the WRC of Beaufort persevered in their work related to fraternity, charity, and loyalty as required by the National organization. They also conducted additional work to uplift their community despite (and because of) the various challenges created by segregation.

A New Chapter:
The Legacy of Fred Washington, Sr.

This chapter details the transition of the historical Beaufort WRC to its contemporary structure. The story behind the decision to formally organize as a charitable organization is provided. The chapter also contains the biography of Fred Washington, Sr., who was designated in 1998 as honorary namesake for the WRC in Beaufort.

A WRC corps in Beaufort is formally documented in the books of the WRC National Conventions from at least 1892[40] (as a detached corps). According to internal records, the WRC in Beaufort operated under that original structure until it was disbanded for a period of time in 1951; the WRC's Journal of the National WRC Convention does resume listing a Beaufort WRC chapter with Mae Dickson as President, Pearl Harsey as Secretary, and Alice E. Lawton as Treasurer in 1960. Most of the organization's activities between 1960 and the early 1990s are not well documented, save for the listing in the WRC's annual convention records each year. Some current members noted that WRC activities waned during the decades following the last "Decoration Day" celebration in Beaufort. This period of time also coincides with the era of intense struggle for voting rights and full equality for African American citizens—the US Civil Rights Era.

---

[40] See appendix for WRC of Beaufort Consolidated Report

During the early 1980s to early 1990s, Black-led community organizations in Beaufort began a revival in many ways, and new initiatives around cultural awareness (such as the Gullah/Geechee Culture) began to take shape. The WRC experienced a similar restart during that time, connected in part with a campaign to restore The Grand Army Hall. The Hall is the physical structure representing the GAR, which was created to ensure continuity of connection for veterans of the US Civil War. The WRC also served as its official auxiliary organization in each locality where a GAR post was located.

Together, GAR posts and their WRC auxiliary corps were responsible for establishing and maintaining the Hall building. The Grand Army Hall in Beaufort was established shortly after David Hunter Post No. 9 purchased property at 706 New Castle Street in 1895. Jim Crow segregation laws meant Beaufort's Black community had limited places to host large events and gatherings; the Grand Army Hall served as one of the main event spaces for the Black community well into the mid-1960s. The building was damaged by a fire and subsequently fell into a state of deterioration, bordering on condemnation by the City of Beaufort.

A committee was organized to restore the building in the early 1980s and established The Grand Army Hall Historic Preservation Foundation chaired by Fred Washington, Sr. As Chairman, he would lead a multi-year fundraising campaign to secure over $72,000 for architectural, engineering, construction and other costs related to the restoration project. Chairman Washington communicated the historically important and present-day implications of the Hall restoration in an appeal letter dated September 29, 1987:

> *"The Grand Army Hall is one of the last physical structures shared by all Blacks in the sea islands of Beaufort. It is fitting for us, during the year that*

we celebrate the 200th birthday of our nation's Constitution, that we remember the old soldiers who lived and died for our union. The battlefield—the long-fought war on poverty, ignorance, and injustice— is here today. We need more help and support to move the forces along."

It is customary for GAR posts and WRC chapters to be named after a soldier. In 1998 the Beaufort Chapter of the Woman's Relief Corps, recognizing the unwavering dedication of Fred Washington, Sr. to the preservation of the Grand Army Hall and his ability to muster community support as well as provide skilled volunteer laborers for duty and service, voted to name the Beaufort WRC in his honor. Fred Washington, Sr. inspired

Fred Washington, Sr.

cohesiveness within the three local auxiliaries to the Grand Army of the Republic and embraced unity as well as commitment in order to achieve a seemingly impossible mission. Under his leadership, the committee comprised of representatives from the Woman's Relief Corps, the Sons and Daughters of Union Civil War Veterans, churches, and other local community groups and fraternal organizations secured the necessary funds for the restoration project, and the newly restored Hall was dedicated on May 30, 1988, during the annual Memorial Day celebration.

Fred Washington, Sr. received Basic Training at Montford Point, NC. Montford Point was the training site for the first African American Marines to enter the Marine Corps; they endured the dehumanizing conditions of segregation and discrimination in the last branch of the US Armed Forces to integrate. He joined the Marine Corps in 1944 and retired in 1970 with the rank of Master Gunnery Sergeant (MGySgt), one of the first African Americans to achieve this rank in the Marine Corps.

The installation service of the newly named Fred Washington, Sr. Woman's Relief Corps No. 1 of SC was conducted by the Woman's Relief Corps National President, Linda Bennett at the Grand Army Hall 706 New Castle Street, Beaufort, SC. This was her first visit to the area. The service was followed by a reception and luncheon at the Hall. During the luncheon Mrs. E. Dalton Singleton, Conductor of the Corps, gave a notable address to the group and guests about Sgt. Washington and his honorable service to our country, his dedication to the betterment of the Beaufort community, and his commitment to the preservation of the Grand Army Hall and its longstanding history of community connectionability for Black residents of Beaufort. The National President expressed her gratitude to the corps for the warm welcome and the gracious hospitality of Gwendolyn G. Jackson (Treasurer) for opening her home to her during her stay.

The 22 members of the Fred Washington, Sr. Woman's Relief Corps No. 1 of SC received its official charter document from the National Organization signed July 26, 1998. From that point forward, the 'Beaufort WRC' became known as the Fred Washington, Sr. Woman's Relief Corps #1 of South Carolina.

A Shared Mission:
Key Partners of the Woman's
Relief Corps

"O heroes 'neath the ocean waves,
While life is strong and true,
With flowers and flags and hearts that love,
We will remember you!"

The mission of the WRC cannot be achieved without the continuous partnership and collaboration of several organizations in Beaufort: a cohort of well-established churches, the Daughters of Union Civil War Veterans, the Sons of Union Civil War Veterans, and the Grand Army Hall. This chapter provides a closer look at those key partners and describes their roles in supporting the work of the WRC.

The Churches

Five local churches have been instrumental in the history and present-day activities of the WRC in Beaufort: Wesley Memorial United Methodist, Tabernacle Baptist, First African Baptist, Grace AME, and Central Baptist Church. In partnership with the WRC membership, these churches co-host

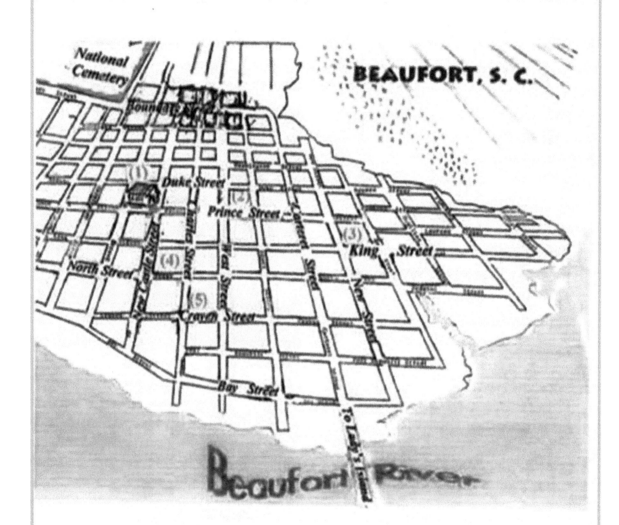

706 NEWCASTLE STREET

BEAUFORT, S. C.

Over 100 Years Old

(1) **The Grand Army Hall** (1896)

(2) **Wesley United Methodist Church** (1833)

(3) **First African Baptist Church** (1865)
           ("Praise House")

(4) **Grace African Methodist Episcopal Church** (1869)
           ("Grace Chapel")

(5) **Tabernacle Baptist Church** (1863)

the annual Memorial Day (Decoration Day) Sunday service on a rotating basis. The Sunday service entailed a processional of WRC members and Daughters of Union Civil War Veteran members led by the Allen Brass Band from the Grand Army Hall building located on New Castle Street, to the designated church co-hosting that year's commemorative program. The order of program included Flag Bearers and the Pledge of Allegiance, musical selections to include The Star Spangled Banner, prayer and scripture, readings of General Logan's Order and Lincoln's Gettysburg Address, and a guest speaker. At the conclusion of the program, the Allen Brass Band led the congregation and other participants on a slow processional to the Waterfront on Bay Street where flowers were thrown in the Beaufort River to commemorate service members who died at sea. The churches are located within blocks of each other in downtown Beaufort. The location of these churches is an important aspect of the WRC's annual services to honor all war dead.

The impact of the faith tradition in the African American community cannot be overstated; from the period of chattel enslavement, during the Reconstruction Era, throughout the period of Jim Crow segregation, and during the Civil Rights Movement of the 1950s and 1960s, the church stood as a cornerstone of power and connectivity for Black families and communities. McKinney (1971) makes it plain in a Harvard Theological Review article: "The Black Church, historically, is the most significant institution in the Black community." Lincoln (1974) provides further support for the cornerstone argument, noting that "In their own churches, in their own denominational structures, Black Christians had become accustomed to a sense of dignity and self-fulfillment impossible to even contemplate in the White church in America. The Black Church created its own literature, established its own publishing houses, elected its own bishops and other administrators, founded its own colleges and seminaries, and developed its own unique style of worship."

The relationship between the cohort of churches and the Beaufort WRC began with the founding of the organization and has continued undiminished since then. In addition to co-hosting the annual Memorial Day (Decoration Day) Sunday program, the Beaufort WRC also works with its partner churches to distribute information and resources to the surrounding communities, to recruit young people to participate in WRC educational programs and activities, and to galvanize the public around the importance of patriotism.

Wesley Memorial United Methodist Church

Founded in 1833 as a mission to enslaved Africans and free Black people in Beaufort, as well as neighboring Lady's Island and St. Helena Island, Wesley Memorial was the first Methodist church in Beaufort. The congregation had both Black and White members from its founding and was first built in the "meeting house" style that was common to the Methodist church.

Wesley Memorial United Methodist Church is a member of the Reconstruction Era National Historic Network, owing to its important role in African American life during that period. The church is documented as one of four places in downtown Beaufort where formerly enslaved people could go to school. After the Civil War, the church persisted as a place of worship for the City's Black residents, developing and supporting leaders who would perform critical social and political roles in the larger community (see Wise & Rowland, June, 2015). Wesley Memorial United Methodist Church is located at 701 West Street, Beaufort, South Carolina.

image source: Najmah Thomas

Tabernacle Baptist Church

Located at 901 Craven Street in downtown Beaufort, the Tabernacle Baptist Church was organized in 1863 as the first formal place of worship for Beaufort's Black residents, who followed the Baptist faith. Construction of the church building is documented as early as 1811 by members who had separated from the Baptist Church of Beaufort.

When Union troops occupied Beaufort in 1861, during the US Civil War, the building became the religious center for African Americans in the city. The Tabernacle Baptist Church congregation purchased the building from the Baptist Church of Beaufort in 1867. Tabernacle's cemetery is the final resting place for famed Civil War hero, state legislator, US Congressman and Grand Army Hall Commander, Robert Smalls. Tabernacle recently launched a capital campaign to build a monument in honor of Harriet Tubman's service in Beaufort during the Civil War and for her leadership role in the Combahee River Raid.

Tabernacle Baptist Church
image source: Najmah Thomas

First African Baptist Church

First African Baptist Church, founded in 1865, grew out of an antebellum Prayer House (also known as a Praise House) for Black members of the Baptist Church of Beaufort. First African Baptists celebrates its founding on January 1, 1865, along with the Emancipation Proclamation.

During the Civil War, and after the Federal occupation of Beaufort, the church was used as a hospital for Black soldiers and also hosted a school for the formerly enslaved. The congregation documents that Civil War hero, state legislator, US Congressman, and delegate to the 1895 SC Constitutional Convention, General Robert Smalls, was baptized at First African Baptist Church on February 5, 1905, under the leadership of Reverend P. Watson. The church is currently located at the same location of the former Prayer House, on the corner of King and New streets in downtown Beaufort.

image source: Najmah Thomas

Grace African Methodist Episcopal Church

The African Methodist Episcopal Church (A.M.E.) is unique among denominations because it was the first in the western world to be founded by and for African-descended people. Richard Allen established a church, in 1878, in protest of the segregated worship of Philadelphia, Pennsylvania's Methodist denomination. The A.M.E., first African American independent religious body, was formally organized in 1816. The roots of Beaufort's Grace A.M.E. Church began in 1858, and the congregation was formally established in 1869. Of the five churches in the cohort of faith-based partners for the Beaufort WRC, Grace A.M.E is the only church that is currently located outside of the downtown Beaufort area. In 2000, the congregation purchased 5.5 acres of land on Lady's Island, SC, and under the leadership of their first woman pastor, Reverend Jeannine R. Smalls, the church achieved its capital fund goals to build new worship facilities off Sam's Point Road.

Old Grace AME Church, image source: WRC records

Central Baptist Church

Central Baptist Church was organized in 1924. It is the 'youngest' of the five local churches that have been instrumental in the history and present-day activities of the Beaufort WRC. Its founding and church activities were documented by the Works Progress Administration (WPA) SC Historical Records Survey in 1936. The church worship services are currently held in the original building, located at 1111 Prince Street.

image source: Najmah Thomas

The Sons & Daughters of Union Veterans of the Civil War

The Beaufort Sons of Union Veterans of the Civil War (SUVCW) is an affiliated membership organization (Edward Wallace Camp No. 21) of the national SUVCW. The organization has a mission of supporting the SUVCW National Organization and also places an emphasis on perpetuating the history and memory of the African American men and women who fought for their freedom during the US Civil War, 1861-1865. It is one of three membership organizations housed at the Grand Army Hall on New Castle Street.

The Beaufort Daughters of Union Veterans of the Civil War (DUVCW) is also an affiliated membership organization of the national DUVCW. The national group is a "not-for-profit organization formed to unite the daughters, granddaughters, great granddaughters, and all female direct lineal descendants of honorably discharged Union Veterans of the Civil War in promoting our principle mission, which is: to perpetuate the memories of our ancestral fathers who served in the Civil War, to honor their loyalty and their unselfish sacrifices to preserve the Union, and to keep alive the history of those who participated in that heroic struggle for the maintenance of our free government." (DUVCW website, 2022)

The Grand Army Hall

The GAR was created to ensure continuity of connection for veterans of the US Civil War, and the WRC was quickly identified as its official auxiliary organization across at the national level and in each locality where a GAR post was located. According to national reports, the WRC of Beaufort regularly reported that the GAR "Post and Corps work in harmony" with each other, as required by national regulations.

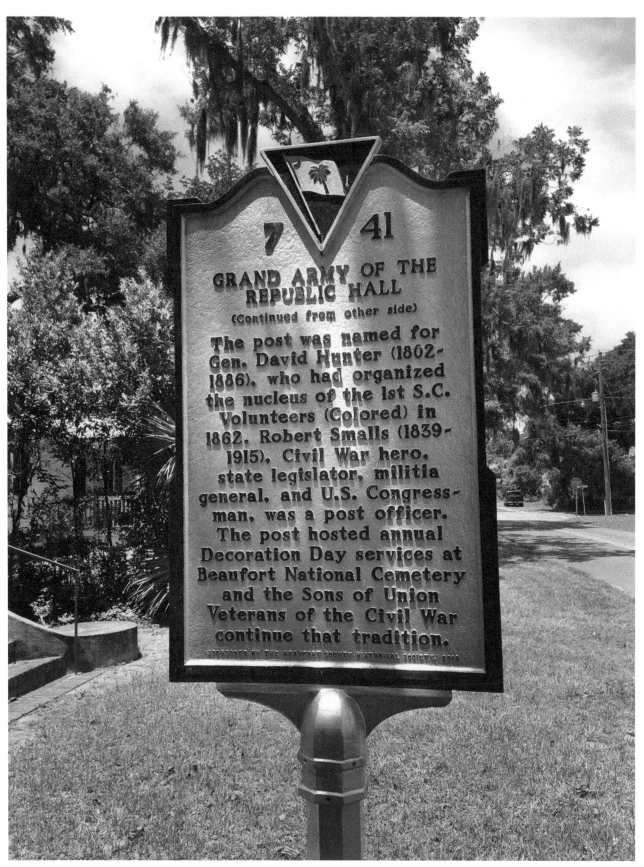

image source: Najmah Thomas

One of the primary responsibilities of that GAR Post coordination was related to the establishment and maintenance of the Grand Army Hall building. Six years following its formal organization, in 1889, GAR Post No. 9 purchased property at 706 New Castle Street in the City of Beaufort and constructed the Grand Army Hall[41]. These structures were erected by Posts across the country to host regular GAR and WRC activities.

As a part of the segregated south, Beaufort's Black community had very few options for public gathering spaces. The Grand Army Hall then served as a nucleus of activity for the Black community, particularly Black soldiers, well into the mid-1960s. The early impact of Post No. 9's WRC auxiliary is evident in that the Hall property on New Castle Street was deeded to the WRC of Beaufort on June 15, 1896, in recognition of their role in raising funds to pay for the building. Today, the structure in Beaufort remains active, housing a mini museum dedicated to the history and memory of Black military personnel. The Grand Army Hall is recorded as the only remaining Civil War structure related to the GAR in South Carolina[42]. It was used in various forms, including as a worship location, in 1940 when author and anthropologist Zora Neale Hurston recorded services at the Grand Army Hall Commandment Keeper Church.

In 1999 the need arose for the maintenance and upkeep of the monthly utility bill payments and annual insurance for the beloved Grand Army Hall. As the Beaufort Woman's Relief Corps had done in the earlier years to provide nursing assistance to the troops and monetary help in paying for the construction of the Grand Army Hall, they again stepped in and provided funds to pay

---

[41]

[42] The Grand Army Hall in Beaufort is the only surviving GAR structure in South Carolina and is one of only two GAR structures for Black veterans in the US. The other Hall, Charles Sumner Post No. 25 is located in Chestertown, Maryland." https://mht.maryland.gov/secure/medusa/PDF/Kent/K-661.pdf ; https://greenbookofsc.com/locations/grand-army-of-the-republic-hall/

image source: Najmah Thomas

image source: Najmah Thomas

the expenses for the Hall beginning in August 2001 and continuing through August 2012.

The FWSr. WRC #1 of Beaufort, SC assumed responsibility for managing rental and usage of the Hall during this period, which offered some small amount of financial support for the building's needs. As a part of this arrangement, the women of the FWSr. WRC #1 of Beaufort, SC were responsible for opening and securing the building after rentals (day and late nights), and for cleaning and ensuring that the building was ready for the next rental. This was often a long and tedious task, but the members saw the need and responded favorably, as they had willingly done in the past.

Eventually, as the Grand Army Hall Committee began to regroup and new leadership roles emerged, the FWSr. WRC #1 of Beaufort, SC was able to relinquish responsibility for the ongoing management and upkeep of the Hall. The three allied groups housed at the hall began to function as a unit once again, sharing ideas and sponsoring joint activities to benefit the Grand Army Hall and the Beaufort community at large.

Someone to March Over Me: Leaders and Members of the Woman's Relief Corps

This chapter offers background information on former and current members of the Woman's Relief Corps in Beaufort and includes a partial list of past and present officers. The chapter provides a glimpse into the lived experiences of several FWSr. WRC #1 of Beaufort, SC members, through excerpts of interviews conducted during the summer of 2019. The chapter also presents the case for ongoing membership and explains why the FWSr. WRC #1 of Beaufort, SC is still a valuable and relevant organization.

Pictured left to right: Julia Ferguson, Delo Washington, Gwendolyn Jackson, Ruth Terry, LaFrance Ferguson, Helen Sanford (who lived to be 100 years old), Addie Marsh and Lucille Culberson (WRC)

The FWSr. WRC #1 of Beaufort, SC commissioned a study to document their history and to help chart their future. A part of the study included oral interviews conducted with several club members and partners. They were asked about their memories of growing up in Beaufort County and earliest recollections of their WRC membership. Interview questions also included the national WRC, the most important aspects about WRC membership, and the future of the FWSr. WRC #1 of Beaufort, SC. Several themes were also revealed as a part of the interview processes. High levels of patriotism were expressed in the interviews, both in terms of pride for families and friends who served and are serving in the armed forces, and in terms of a sense of connection to the country. Current members (some who have been a part of the WRC for more than 50 years) provided their perspectives on patriotism, and their responses support findings in the research about Black Southern women's commitment to symbolic patriotism:

> *"Patriotism is allegiance to those values found in the Declaration, the Constitution, and the Civil War Amendments; it means freedom for all people. **We were freedom fighters**; we were encouraged to speak out as though we were just as important as anyone else. We supported the veterans and the ideals and values that were being promoted after the Civil War."*

> *"We've always, I've felt, been patriotic; my father and a lot of people in the Beaufort area enlisted...during the Civil War we fought with the Union. **This is America, and this is our country**...and if we don't stand for something, then it seems as if we are falling for anything. This is my country; it has worked for me."*

Other responses spoke to the balancing act between patriotism and dealing with Jim Crow segregation:

*"Because the South was segregated at that time, and there was so little recognition of who we were and what we contributed to this town, **we were proud of those guys, even though some people looked at military service as 'slave sacrifice'**...the group existed and they did a lot to help the Black community, military interaction with members in the community... we sponsored events for Parris Island because there was nothing for Blacks who were in the military to do. It was our presence that combatted the mentality against Black patriotism."*

*"Rain or shine...we remembered those who served and sacrificed their lives. I had one sister and four brothers who served. My sister wanted to go in [to] the Navy, but at the time, they were not taking Blacks. I figured **so many of us had mothers and fathers who were having a hard time, so the kids went in the service."***

*"Being in the military in the 1950s, there was prejudice, but I wanted to get out [of Beaufort]. I think it is much better now than it used to be. **If we don't participate, it is not because we can't**; the offer is on the table."*

Responses also captured the level of pride these women have for the work they and their corps members did in the name of patriotism:

*"We should be proud of what we've accomplished in the past...**these women were strong women in our own community**."*

*"**I loved to carry that stick** [the American Flag]. When something happened to a member, we stuck with them. All those people, we marched over them; I marched over them. Who's gonna march over me?"*

The story of the WRC in Beaufort is a timely reminder that Black women in the South have carried the banner of patriotism since the country's founding and continue to do so in the present day. This is a truly unique example of a women's

Larcena Laurie, Sheldonia Washington, Dora Pigler and other WRC members
Image source: WRC records

club that aspired to unite the Black South, as a part of the national community, in a space and time where Black people were being purposely written out of the national narrative. Despite its complicated relationship with the National WRC, as an all-Black 'detached corps,' these women were able to leverage the national mission and accomplish goals above and beyond those parameters in order to benefit the Black community in Beaufort. Moreover, they were able to help instill a strong sense of military pride and patriotism within the Black community.

The Present and Future of the FWSr. WRC #1 of Beaufort, SC

On the surface, this may seem like an organization that is primarily concerned with the past and mainly for the Elders in the community. But the three objectives (perpetuating the memory of the GAR; providing assistance to veterans, their widows and orphans; and promoting patriotism) are still very relevant in the present and valuable for the future. The FWSr. WRC #1 of Beaufort, SC is still actively engaged in the telling of that story through its current activities at the community and national level.

The Fred Washington, Sr. Woman's Relief Corps No. 1 of SC community involvement and visibility:

- Sponsors the Sunday Memorial Service, which is held at a different church in the vicinity of the Grand Army Hall and the Memorial Service to the Sailor- Soldier Dead at Beaufort Water Front. In 2013 the corps decided to begin to identify a veteran in the community or corps to honor for their service to our country or this corps at each Sunday Memorial Service.

- Sponsors oratory contests, involving school-age students. Winner awarded monetary gift and selected to deliver Lincoln's Gettysburg Address for

Sunday Memorial Service. Announcements are sent to schools and churches for participants and through word-of-mouth.

- Active participants in the annual Memorial Day (also remembered as "Decoration Day") Parade and Memorial Day Service at the Beaufort National Cemetery.

- Service on Beaufort Veterans Day Committee

- Sponsors educational lectures and display exhibits at the Grand Army Hall for adults and children

- Awards scholarships to students

- Provides presentations for the Beaufort Gullah Festival

Contest Winner Elizabeth Veasey, 1999

- Co-sponsors of in the annual "Remembering Decoration Day" event by the Beaufort County Community Center. This is an outdoor event held at the Washington Street Park geared to free family fun with games, entertainment, showcasing local group and individual talent, food, and lots of prizes. (Our organization set-up and directed activity event tent and informational display.)

The Fred Washington, Sr. Woman's Relief Corps No. 1 of SC national Woman's Relief Corps visibility:

- In August, 2014 Corp President, Alice Washington attended the National Convention in Springfield, IL
- Corps members have served on National Appointed Committees

WRC Members (L to R): Louise Hearon, Lucille Culberson, Alice Veasey, Barbara Glaze,LaFrance Ferguson, and Addie Marsh
image source: WRC records

Despite their continued service, the interviews revealed that the Fred Washington, Sr. Woman's Relief Corps No. 1 of SC members are unanimous in their desire to sustain the organization by recruiting and retaining younger members. Members expressed a willingness to continue active service but acknowledged concerns associated with aging/health issues that may prevent them from participating as much as they had in the past:

> *"We want to do, but we are not able to do. I've done what I can do…we can't be selfish.* **We have to let young people lead; if not, it is going to fade out.***"*

The case for continuing membership (and perhaps a revival effort) can easily be made when we examine the current state of discourse around patriotism and democracy, and even the difficulties that some veterans experience when returning to the community after service. Several of the members provided valuable suggestions for strategies to recruit and increase membership, particularly among younger members and youth.

These suggestions can be categorized in terms of activities, partnerships, and information:

- Activities
  - Host an open house and/or breakfast gathering at the Grand Army Hall
  - Do more visiting with veterans and take young people along
  - Host fun activities for youth on a regular basis

- Partnerships
  - Have the Grand Army Hall open more than one day a week
  - Work on a rotating schedule between the three groups (Sons, Daughters and WRC)
  - Recruit from local families with veterans and on local military bases

- Information
  - Educate our current members so they can recruit with confidence
  - Host a website so young people can access information

A new generation of youth and young adults in Beaufort would be well-served by exposure to the WRC's perspectives and by a stronger connection to the Grand Army Hall. Despite significant progress made, from the Reconstruction Era to the Civil Rights Movement and beyond, traditional history courses still often fail to connect with some in Beaufort's African American community. Membership in an organization dedicated to lifting stories off the pages of history and linking those

Ethel Washington, Gwendolyn Jackson, Bertha Smith and other WRC members lead Woman's Relief Corps Memorial Service to Sailor-Soldier Dead at Beaufort, SC Water Front
image source: WRC records

stories with familiar faces and places could have a positive and lasting impact. It is worth noting that ours is still a very young nation; its history—our story—must be told and told again, imagined and reimagined, for usefulness in the current context. The Fred Washington, Sr. Woman's Relief Corps #1 of Beaufort, SC is one extraordinary way to share our nation's story with the next generation.

WRC members Barbara Glaze & Alice Veasey (Beaufort National Cemetery 2009)

DUVCW and Alice Veasey (WRC) at Beaufort National Cemetery

Fred Washington Sr. Woman's Relief Corps, Sons and Daughters of Union Veterans of the
Civil War Float (Memorial Day Parade 2015 – Beaufort, SC)

WRC members Alice Washington (President), Linda Robinson, Fredrica Cooper and Barbara
Glaze at Memorial Day Observance Beaufort National Cemetery 2022

WRC members Alice Veasey, Linda Robinson, Fredrica Cooper, Barbara Glaze, and Alice Washington (President) with DUVCW members at the Beaufort National Cemetery, Memorial Day 2022

Afterward:
A Public History Website
WomansReliefCorpsBeaufort.org

The FWSr. WRC #1 of Beaufort, SC commissioned a study to document and share their history with current and future members, as well as with the community at large. This effort constitutes a work of 'public history' ("an intentional application of historical methodology outside of academic settings", Kelley, R., 1978). Categories of public history can include living history museums, archives and libraries, historic landmarks, as well as oral history projects.

The FWSr. WRC #1 of Beaufort, SC was already engaged in the creation of public history prior to the publication of this book; the Grand Army Hall is a museum, library and historic landmark all-in-one, and the interviews conducted as a part of the documentation process were also recorded as oral histories. This book constitutes another tangible public history product, and in an effort to share this remarkable story with a wider audience, The FWSr. WRC #1 of Beaufort, SC also authorized development of a companion website (www.womansreliefcorpsbeaufort.org). This website contains historical documents, photos and other exhibits, as well as audio files; the site also provides information on upcoming activities, as well as membership application process and requirements.

Website Exhibits

Administration & Organizational

National WRC Charter Letter

IRS 501(c)3 Certificate

SC State Corporation Commission Certificate

Initiation/Ceremonial Descriptions/Rites/Rituals

Meeting Minutes

Membership Rosters

Correspondence (external)

Local to membership; local to external; national

Daughters/Sons of Civil War Veterans

Decoration Day & Memorial Day

State/Federal Resolution

Decoration Day History

Grand Army Hall

David Hunter Post #9 Real Estate records

Restoration Committee Records

WRC National Convention Records

1891-2021 Consolidated Report

References

Beaufort County Department of Veterans Affairs (1989). *"From the Pages of History": May 29, 1989 Memorial Day Program*. Beaufort, SC: Intsty Prints.

Blight, D. W. (1989). "For Something beyond the Battlefield": Frederick Douglass and the Struggle for the Memory of the Civil War. *The Journal of American History, 75*:4, 1156-1178.

Blight, D. W. (2019). *The First Decoration Day*. The Zinn Education Project https://www.zinnedproject.org/materials/the-first-decoration-day.

Booker, S. (1969). Susie King Taylor Civil War Nurse. New York, NY: McGraw-Hill Book Company.

Burton, O. V. & Cross, W. (2014) Penn Center: A History Preserved. Athens, GA: The University of Georgia Press.

Clyburn, J. E. (2014). Blessed Experiences: Genuinely Southern, Proudly Black. Columbia, SC: The University of South Carolina Press.

Busby, M. (Ed.). (1992) Daughters of Africa: An International Anthology of Words and Writings by Women of African Descent from the Ancient Egyptian to the Present. New York City, NY: Pantheon Books.

Davies, W. E. (1947). The Problem of Race Segregation in the Grand Army of the Republic. *The Journal of Southern History, 13*:3, 354-372.

Fahs, A. (1999). The Feminized Civil War: Gender, Northern Popular Literature, and the Memory of the War, 1861-1900. *The Journal of American History, 85:4,* 1461-1494.

Fears, M. L. J. (2004). Civil Way and Living History Reenacting about "People of Color": How to Begin, What to Wear, Why Reenact. Westminister, MD: Heritage Books.

Forten, C. L. (1953). The Journal of Charlotte L. Forten: A young black women's reactions to the white world of the Civil War era. Billington, R. A. (Introduction and Ed.). New York, NY: Norton & Company.

Gannon, B. A. (2014). The Won Cause: Black and White Comradeship in the Grand Army of the Republic. Chapel Hill, NC, https://doi.org/10.5149/9780807877708_gannon. CHAPTER 4 – THE BLACK GAR CIRCLE.

Janney, C. (2013). Remembering the Civil War: Reunion and the Limits of Reconciliation. Chapel Hill, NC: University of North Carolina Press.

Kelley, R. (1978). Public History: Its Origins, Nature, and Prospects. *The Public Historian, 1*(1), 16–28. https://doi.org/10.2307/3377666

Kennedy, J.C. (2015). Race, Civil War Memory, and Sisterhood in the Woman's Relief Corps. *Proceedings of the Third Conference on Veterans in Society,* Roanoke, VA

Lebsock, S. (1985). The Free Women of Petersburg: Status and Culture in a Southern Town, 1784-1860. New York City: NY, Norton & Company.

Lincoln, C. E. (1974). The power in the Black Church. *CrossCurrents, 24*(1), 3–21. http://www.jstor.org/stable/24457876

McCoy, Cameron (2011) Jim Crow America and The Marines Of Montford Point In The World War Ii Era. A Thesis submitted to the Office of Graduate Studies of Texas A&M University in partial fulfillment of the requirements for the degree of Master of Arts.

McKinney, R. (1971). The Black Church: Its Development and Present Impact. *Harvard Theological Review,* 64(4), 452-481. doi:10.1017/S0017816000023397

McLaurin, M. A. (2009). The Marines of Montford Point: America's First Black Marines. The Marines of Montford Point - Google Books.

Morgan, F. (2005). Women and Patriotism in Jim Crow America. Chapel Hill, NC: The University of North Carolina Press.

Morris, J. B. (2017). Yes, Lord, I Know the Road. Columbia, SC: The University of South Carolina Press.

Mosley, E. S. (2021). Footprints of the Montford Point Marines. A Narrative of the Epic Strides in Overcoming the Racial Disparities of the United States Marine Corps. Footprints of the Montford Point Marines - Google Books

Nussbaum, M. C. (2012). Teaching patriotism: Love and critical freedom. *U. Chi. L. Rev., 79,* 213.

Parker, C. S. (2010). Symbolic versus Blind Patriotism: Distinction without Difference? Political Research Quarterly, 63(1), 97–114. https://doi.org/10.1177/1065912908327228

Preston, E. (1906). Patriotism in the Public Schools. *The Journal of Education, 63:*18, 486-487.

Rauch, M. T. (1947). The First Memorial Day. *Journal of the Illinois State Historical Society (1908-1984), 40:*2, 213-216.

Rood, H. W. (1923). The Grand Army of the Republic. *The Wisconsin Magazine of History, 6:*4, 403-413.

Smith, Rogers M. 1988. The American Creed and American Identity: The Limits of Liberal Citizenship in the United States. *Western Political Quarterly* 41: 225-241.

Societies of the War of the Rebellion (1906). *The Journal of Education,* 63:17, 458, 468.

Taylor, K. S. (1902). Reminiscences of my Life in Camp with the 33rd U.S. Colored Troops, Late 1st South Carolina Volunteers. Romero, P.W. & Rose, W. L. (Eds.). Princeton, NJ: Markus Wiener Publishers.

Washington, D. (2013). Grand Army Hall Women and a Sense of Community. *Paper presented at the annual meeting of the Association for the Study of African American Life and History*, Atlanta, GA.

Woman's Relief Corps (1984). Rules and Regulations of the Governance of Woman's Relief Corps Auxiliary to the Grand Army of the Republic. Boston, MA: E. B. Stillings & Co.

Woman's Relief Corps Department of Massachusetts (1895). History of the Department of Massachusetts Woman's Relief Corps, Auxiliary to the Grand Army of the Republic. Boston, MA: E. B. Stillings & Co.

Woman's Relief Corps (U.S.), National Convention. (1912-1923). *Journal of the...National Convention of the Woman's Relief Corps.* Boston, MA: E. B. Stillings & Co.

About Najmah Thomas, PhD

Najmah Thomas, PhD, is a full-time Associate Professor in the Human Services Program and a faculty member for African American Studies at the University of South Carolina Beaufort. She earned a BA in Public Policy at the College of William and Mary, a Masters of Adult Education and Distance Learning from the University of Phoenix, and a PhD in Public Policy and Administration (urban policy) at Virginia Commonwealth University. Her career includes serving as Deputy Director for the Crater Regional Workforce Investment Board, Director of Capacity Building for the Cameron Foundation, and Policy Planning Specialist for the Virginia Community College System. She has published several articles and secured numerous grants. A Southeastern Council of Foundations Hull Fellow, she received the Living Legacy Award from the Association for the Study of African American Life and History. She is also a 2017 Fellow with the Institute for African American Research at USC. Najmah Thomas lives in the Beaufort area with her family.

Fresh Ink Group

Independent Multi-media Publisher

Fresh Ink Group / Push Pull Press

Voice of Indie / GeezWriter

✍

Hardcovers

Softcovers

All Ebook Formats

Audiobooks

Podcasts

Worldwide Distribution

✍

Indie Author Services

Book Development, Editing, Proofing

Graphic/Cover Design

Video/Trailer Production

Website Creation

Social Media Marketing

Writing Contests

Writers' Blogs

✍

Authors

Editors

Artists

Experts

Professionals

✍

FreshInkGroup.com

info@FreshInkGroup.com

Twitter: @FreshInkGroup

Facebook.com/FreshInkGroup

LinkedIn: Fresh Ink Group

Fresh Ink Group
FreshInkGroup.com